Cause & Effect:
The Fall of Rome

Don Nardo

San Diego, CA

© 2016 ReferencePoint Press, Inc.
Printed in the United States

For more information, contact:
ReferencePoint Press, Inc.
PO Box 27779
San Diego, CA 92198
www. ReferencePointPress.com

LIBRARY OF CONGRESS CATALOGING-IN-PUBLICATION DATA

Nardo, Don, 1947-
  Cause & effect : the fall of Rome / by Don Nardo.
    pages cm. -- (Cause & effect in history)
  Includes bibliographical references and index.
  Audience: Grade 9 to 12.
  ISBN-13: 978-1-60152-794-3 (hardback)
  ISBN-10 1-60152-794-2 (hardback)
  1. Rome--History--Empire, 284-476--Juvenile literature. I. Title. II. Title: Fall of Rome.
  DG311.N264 2015
  937'.09--dc23
                                                        2015002424

CONTENTS

"History is a complex study of the many causes that have influenced happenings of the past and the complicated effects of those varied causes."

—William & Mary School of Education,
Center for Gifted Education

Understanding the causes and effects of historical events is rarely simple. The fall of Rome, for instance, had many causes. The onslaught of barbarians from the north, the weakening of Rome's economic and military foundations, and internal disunity are often cited as contributing to Rome's collapse. Yet even when historians generally agree on a primary cause (in this instance, the barbarian invasions) leading to a specific outcome (that is, Rome's fall), they also agree that other conditions at the time influenced the course of those events. Under different conditions, the effect might have been something else altogether.

The value of analyzing cause and effect in history, therefore, is not necessarily to identify a single cause for a singular event. The real value lies in gaining a greater understanding of history as a whole and being able to recognize the many factors that give shape and direction to historic events. As outlined by the National Center for History in the Schools at the University of California–Los Angeles, these factors include "the importance of the individual in history . . . the influence of ideas, human interests, and beliefs; and . . . the role of chance, the accidental and the irrational."

ReferencePoint's Cause & Effect in History series examines major historic events by focusing on specific causes and consequences. For instance, in *Cause & Effect: The French Revolution*, a chapter explores how inequality led to the revolution. And in *Cause & Effect: The American Revolution*, one chapter delves into this question: "How did assistance from France help the American cause?" Every book in the series includes thoughtful discussion of questions like these—supported by facts, examples, and a mix of fully documented primary and secondary source quotes. Each title also includes an overview of the event so that readers have a broad context for understanding the more detailed discussions of specific causes and their effects.

The value of such study is not limited to the classroom; it can also be applied to many areas of contemporary life. The ability to analyze and interpret history's causes and consequences is a form of critical thinking. Critical thinking is crucial in many professions, ranging from law enforcement to science. Critical thinking is also essential for developing an educated citizenry that fully understands the rights and obligations of living in a free society. The ability to sift through and analyze complex processes and events and identify their possible outcomes enables people in that society to make important decisions.

The *Cause & Effect in History* series has two primary goals. One is to help students think more critically about history and develop a true understanding of its complexities. The other is to help build a foundation for those students to become fully participating members of the society in which they live.

IMPORTANT EVENTS LEADING TO ROME'S FALL

BCE 27
After a long series of civil wars that have decimated the Republic, the young political strongman Octavian takes the name of Augustus. This marks the start of a new, more autocratic realm—the Roman Empire.

180
Death of the thoughtful, constructive emperor Marcus Aurelius and the beginning of the Empire's gradual downward economic and political spiral.

284
The emperor Diocletian institutes major political, social, and military reforms, saving the Empire from utter collapse.

BCE 700 / CE 150   200   250

BCE 753
Traditional founding date for the city-state of Rome.

235
The Empire enters a period in which it nearly crumbles under the effects of debilitating wars and widespread political anarchy and civil strife.

BCE 509
The leading Roman landowners throw out their last king and establish the Roman Republic.

307
Reign of the emperor Constantine I begins; he continues the reforms begun by Diocletian and befriends the long-persecuted Christians.

CE 98
Reign of the emperor Trajan begins, marking a period in which the Roman Empire reaches its zenith of power and size.

378
The Visigoths devastatingly defeat the Eastern Roman emperor, Valens, at Adrianople in northern Greece.

ca. 407
Rome's distant province in Britain falls under the control of migrating barbarian tribes.

476
German-born general Odoacer forces the young emperor Romulus Augustulus from his throne, after which the Western Empire's government ceases to exist. The Eastern Empire, however, survives in Constantinople.

568
Another barbarian tribe, the Lombards, takes control of northern and central Italy.

350   450   550   /   1450

375
The Huns, a warlike nomadic people from central Asia, pour into eastern Europe, forcing the Goths and other barbarian peoples into Rome's northern provinces.

455
Rome is overrun and sacked once more, this time by the Vandals.

1453
The Ottoman Turks besiege and take control of Constantinople, marking the official end of the last remnant of the Roman Empire.

410
Commanded by their war chief, Alaric, the Visigoths capture and loot the city of Rome.

395
On the death of the emperor Theodosius I, his two sons rule from separate cities, permanently dividing the Empire roughly in half.

Rome's Fall in the Undergrowth of History

Throughout recorded history, the major events that have shaped the human story have depended in large degree on the occurrence and timing of the many smaller events that caused them. That reality forces one to consider an intriguing alternative. Namely, what might have happened if one of the smaller incidents that brought about a particular major event had taken place at a different time or not occurred at all? In such a case, historians point out, the major event in question would not have happened. Or at least it would not have transpired in the same manner or at the specific time that history records.

Noted American military historian Robert Cowley cites the example of a well-known major historical event—the American Revolution. Among the numerous smaller events that added up to make the formation of the United States possible, he points out, were "small accidents" and "split-second decisions." Consider, Cowley says, "the sudden fog on the East River that allowed George Washington and his badly beaten army to escape to Manhattan after the Battle of Long Island in the summer of 1776." Without that fog, "Washington might have been trapped on Brooklyn Heights and forced to surrender. Would there have been a United States if that had happened?" Cowley adds, "Few events have been more dependent on 'what ifs' than the American Revolution. We are the product of a future that might not have been."[1]

What If Rome Had Survived?

No less major an event in humanity's long saga was the fall of the Western Roman Empire in the late 400s and early 500s CE. The consensus of modern scholars is that many factors—including economic, political, and social ones—contributed to that epic historical milestone. But the largest single cause of Rome's fall, they agree, was the onrush of an enormous tide of northern European tribes, the barbarians.

This immense threat materialized at a time when the Roman army was no longer the extraordinarily powerful military force it had been in prior centuries. That army had once been huge, disciplined, and deadly. But it had already lost much of its punch when it faced a monstrous swarm of Visigoths at Adrianople (in what is now Turkey) in 378. After

The towering civilization that was ancient Rome (pictured) eventually collapsed under the weight of a mix of economic, political, and social factors. Possibly the greatest threat came from the onslaught of outsiders who benefited from the weakened state of Rome's once-powerful military.

crushing Rome's forces there, the Visigoths and other barbarians steadily hammered away at and occupied the outer Roman provinces. Eventually, the once vast Western Roman realm shrank until all that was left was Italy and a few fragments of some nearby provinces. By then Rome's fate was sealed. It was fairly easy for a barbarian general to send the last Roman emperor into permanent retirement and declare himself king of Italy.

However, as Cowley states, "it did not have to be that way."[2] Cornell University scholar Barry S. Strauss agrees, saying there definitely could have been "a different result if just a few changes are imagined."[3] First, what if the timing of these events had been different? Imagine, for instance, that those full-scale barbarian invasions had happened earlier, when the Roman army was far stronger, more disciplined, and more effective. In that case Rome may well have had the fortitude to beat back the barbarian hordes.

A Roman America?

Strauss also explores a more specific incident—the Romans' decisive defeat at Adrianople. Even if the timing of the barbarian invasions had been the same, he says, under somewhat different circumstances the Roman army would not have grown weaker and less disciplined before that key battle. In that case Roman forces would likely have won the day. That "would have bought Rome time to regroup," Strauss writes. "It might, moreover, have generated the confidence and political will to ram through the political and military reforms needed to man the Roman army."[4]

Based on these suppositions, Strauss asks, "What if the Roman Empire had survived?" One likely answer, he argues, is that it "would have remained a great power dominating a huge area." Furthermore, "Latin-speaking Europe, governed from a capital in Italy, would have become a more orderly and stable society than the boisterous and freedom-loving Germanic kingdoms that replaced imperial Rome." As a result, Strauss suggests, the medieval Europe of the existing history books would not have arisen. In turn, "there would have been no feudalism, no knights, no chivalry." Similarly, he asks, in that very different Roman-ruled Europe, would Columbus "have sailed across the

Atlantic?" This "is a good question," Strauss admits, "but one thing is certain: A new Roman Empire in the Americas would have been far less dedicated to individual liberty than the English colonies turned out to be."[5]

An Infinity of Options

None of these alternative historical scenarios actually happened, of course. The facts are that the Roman army lost the fight at Adrianople; the last Roman emperor, Romulus Augustulus, did indeed go into forced retirement; the medieval era filled the vacuum left by Rome's demise; and Columbus and other European explorers did open up large-scale exploitation of the Americas.

Yet examining what might have been if one or two incidents had happened earlier or not at all sharpens human understanding of the flow of history. Looking at alternate possibilities, Cowley asserts, demonstrates how random, unpredictable, and decidedly unwritten historical events are. Everything that has ever taken place, including Rome's fall, has been contingent on many factors. Any one of them depended on numerous other random happenings and therefore could easily have occurred differently.

> "A new Roman Empire in the Americas would have been far less dedicated to individual liberty than the English colonies turned out to be."[5]
>
> —Cornell University scholar Barry S. Strauss.

Thus, Cowley concludes, "much as we like to think otherwise, outcomes are no more certain in history than they are in our own lives. If nothing else, the diverging tracks in the undergrowth of history celebrate the infinity of human options. The road not taken belongs on the map."[6]

A Brief History of Rome's Rise and Fall

Just as Rome endured a calamitous and regrettable fall, it also enjoyed a calm and hopeful rise. What was destined to become one of the world's biggest and most important empires was born along the fast-moving Tiber River not far from Italy's western coast. There, in about 1000 BCE, small villages appeared atop seven low hills near a sharp bend in the river. The evidence for these settlements includes several pottery and bronze utensils and some graves containing urns filled with the cremated remains of the inhabitants.

As for who these folk were and where they came from, historians are still a bit uncertain. One possibility is that those prehistoric villagers were native to central Italy, an offshoot of the Apennine culture. Modern experts named it after the rugged mountain range that runs north–south through the Italian boot. Members of that society used tools and weapons made of bronze (an alloy of copper and tin) and practiced inhumation, or burial of the dead.

A second theory identifies those earliest Romans as members of Latin-speaking tribes that came from somewhere in southeastern Europe. The traditional view is that they entered Italy sometime in the second millennium BCE and steadily made their way across the peninsula. Finally, some of them erected those villages on the hills overlooking the Tiber.

Eventually, the settlements in question coalesced, or came together, into a single town called Rome. This occurrence may well be what the later Romans remembered as their traditional founding event, which they dated to 753 BCE. Indeed, historians do think that the hilltop villages coalesced in about 700 BCE, give or take a few decades.

The Flexible, Popular Republic

Initially, Rome was ruled by a series of kings, as were other city-states in central Italy at the time. (A typical ancient city-state was a central urban area surrounded by supporting farmlands and villages.) In roughly 509 BCE, however, the leading citizens expelled their last king and founded a new government and state—the Roman Republic. Citizens of that state were then able to vote for their leaders, including two consuls who served jointly as chief administrators for a year. Yet

Roman soldiers lead captives in a triumphal procession. Rome's highly skilled and disciplined army contributed to the Empire's success and longevity as a dominant world power.

"Cities Shine in Radiance"

Rome reached its political and cultural zenith in the second century CE. At the time, one of the more common literary forms was the panegyric, a highly formal speech praising a leader, country, or empire. The noted Greek writer Aelius Aristides delivered one in the middle years of that century. It summed up Rome's achievement, in Aristides' words, of unifying and expertly administering the peoples of the known world. All those peoples "speak in unison," he began, "in praying this Empire may last for all time. All everywhere are ruled equally." He went on:

> Every place is full of gymnasia, fountains, gateways, temples, shops, and schools. [Moreover] gifts never stop flowing from you to the cities, and because of your imperial generosity to all, the leading beneficiaries cannot be determined. Cities shine in radiance and beauty, and the entire countryside is decked out like a pleasure ground, [and so] only those outside your Empire, if there are any, are fit to be pitied for losing such blessings. [That means that] Greek and barbarian can now readily go wherever they please with their property or without it. It is just like going from their own to their own country. . . . For safety, it is enough to be a Roman, or rather, one of your subjects, [because] you have surveyed the whole world, built bridges of all sorts across rivers, cut down mountains to make paths for chariots, filled the deserts with hostels, and civilized it all with system and order.

Aelius Aristides, *Roman Panegyric,* in *Roman Civilization, Sourcebook II: The Empire,* ed. Naphtali Lewis and Meyer Reinhold. New York: Harper and Row, 1966, pp. 101, 138.

the new government was mainly controlled by the Senate, a legislative body composed of well-to-do nobles. They crafted the policies the consuls acted on.

The Roman commoners, called plebs, came to feel that the nobles held too much power. So over time those commoners won the right to elect their own officials, called tribunes. They had the power to veto any law made by the nobles.

This republican system proved both flexible and popular. It served the practical, hardworking Romans well and was one of the three main causes of the Roman state's swift expansion in power and influence in the centuries that followed. A second major basis for Rome's early success was that it developed an increasingly skilled and disciplined army that rarely lost a battle. (Moreover, when the Roman military *did* lose, it learned from its mistakes and came back stronger than ever.)

The third cause of Rome's remarkable early expansion was the wise, lenient way it dealt with its defeated enemies. Most often, the triumphant Romans introduced the Latin language to former adversaries, along with Roman ideas, laws, and customs. That way these peoples became allies who were eventually Romanized and absorbed into the growing Roman realm. Indeed, the Romans possessed an astonishing "talent for patient political reasonableness that was unique in the ancient world," the late, noted historian Michael Grant wrote. "On the whole," Rome kept "its bargains with its allies, displaying a self-restraint, a readiness to compromise, and a calculated generosity that the world had never seen."[7]

With these extraordinary qualities, the Roman realm continually overcame difficult odds, prospered, and grew. By the late 200s BCE, all of Italy had come under Rome's sway, and a mere century and a half later it controlled all the peoples dwelling along the shores of the Mediterranean Sea. This remarkable new political reality prompted many Romans to conceitedly call that vast waterway *mare nostrum*, or "our sea."

Rise of the Empire

In the first century BCE, however, a major chink appeared in the Republic's seemingly invincible armor. Over time some of Rome's military generals had grown unusually powerful. Increasingly, they amassed personal armies more loyal to them than to the state. In the early to mid-first century BCE, several of these military titans, including the famous Julius Caesar, boldly challenged the government. As a result, a series of devastating civil wars rocked the Mediterranean world. Hundreds of thousands of people died, and the survivors were left war-weary and afraid.

This uniquely distressing situation left the Roman world vulnerable to exploitation by a benevolent dictator, an all-powerful ruler who would use his great powers to restore order. That concept was not lost on the shrewd and ambitious victor of the final civil war. Caesar's adopted son, Octavian, solidified his power by appeasing all social groups. He lavishly funded public programs that distributed free food to the poor, for example. He also won over the better-off classes with financial bribes and promises of peace and prosperity. As the first-century-CE Roman historian Tacitus put it, Octavian "seduced the army with bonuses, and his cheap food policy was successful bait for civilians. Indeed, he attracted everybody's good will by the enjoyable gift of peace, then he gradually pushed ahead and absorbed the functions of the Senate, the officials, and even the laws."[8]

Indeed, the Romans heaped so many powers and honors on Octavian that it became only a small final step for the Senate to rename him Augustus, "the exalted one." In retrospect, this ceremony, enacted in 27 BCE, simply confirmed what everyone knew was already true. A new, more autocratic state had replaced the Republic. Augustus never used the title of emperor, but he proved to be the first in a long line of rulers of what came to be called the Roman Empire.

Prosperity and Relative Peace

Despite his being an absolute dictator, Augustus turned out to be an extremely thoughtful, effective ruler—in fact, one of history's finest. Most of his immediate successors turned out to be caring, efficient leaders as well. The result was that the Roman-ruled Mediterranean sphere enjoyed more than two centuries of prosperity and relative peace.

Especially competent and enlightened were the so-called five good emperors—Nerva, Trajan, Hadrian, Antoninus Pius, and Marcus Aurelius. In the midst of their successive rule, lasting from 96 to 180 CE, the Empire was bigger than it had ever been, or ever would be. It extended from the Persian Gulf in the east to the Atlantic Ocean in the west, and from central Britain in the north to northern Africa in the south. That truly enormous imperial realm covered some 3.5 million square miles (9 million sq. km) and held more than 100 million people.

The Height of the Roman Empire, 117 CE

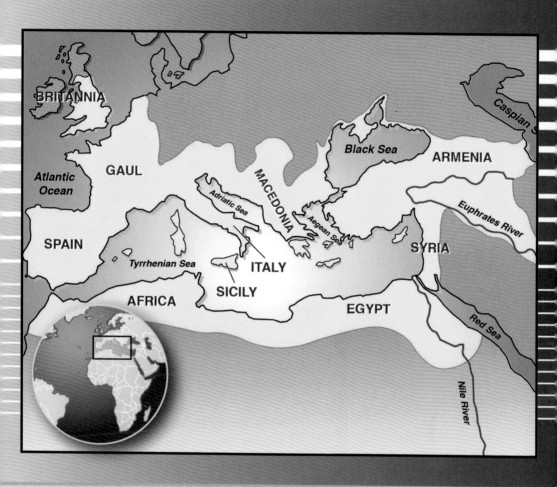

The five good emperors also lifted Roman civilization to its economic, political, and cultural pinnacle. The great eighteenth-century British historian Edward Gibbon famously summed up their achievement. "If a man were called upon," he said, "to fix the period in the history of the world during which the condition of the human race was most happy and prosperous, he would without hesitation name that which elapsed from the accession of Nerva to the death of Aurelius." Gibbon added, "Their united reigns are possibly the only period of history in which the happiness of a great people was the sole object of government."[9]

The Verge of Collapse

It was during the reign of Marcus Aurelius's son, Commodus (ruled 180–192 CE), that Rome's fortunes first got off on the wrong path. It was not simply that Commodus was a self-centered, frivolous leader who was removed from power by an assassin. Most of the emperors who immediately succeeded him were also poor rulers. That political predicament was made worse by the onset of increasingly dire economic conditions; misery, fear, and depopulation caused by disease epidemics; and the appearance of Germanic invaders along the Empire's northern borders and Persian armies on the eastern ones.

The overall result was nearly a century of debilitating and seemingly relentless problems that brought the realm to the very verge of collapse. Modern scholars have variously called it the Anarchy, the century of crisis, and the military monarchy. Whatever one chooses to call the period, its severity is well illustrated by the shocking turnover of leaders at the highest level. Between 235 and 284 alone, more than fifty men claimed to be emperor. No more than half of them had any legal right to the throne, and all but one suffered violent deaths, either by assassination or while fighting the invaders.

> "Their united reigns are possibly the only period of history in which the happiness of a great people was the sole object of government."[9]
>
> —Historian Edward Gibbon on Rome's so-called five good emperors.

However, just when it looked as if all was lost for the once great Roman Empire, a handful of those many imperial claimants rose to the challenge and rescued the realm from certain doom. "In one of the most striking reversals in world history," Grant aptly states it, "Rome's foes were hurled back by a series of formidable military emperors."[10] These tireless soldier-rulers were Claudius II, Aurelian, Probus, and Carus. From 268 to 284, they both drove the invaders back over the borders and crushed the remaining illegal claimants to the throne.

Diocletian's Reforms

Then came Diocletian, the most talented and capable ruler the Romans had known since Marcus Aurelius's death just over a century before. Taking charge of the badly damaged Roman domains in 284,

Among the many so-called barbarian groups that took part in Europe's gigantic folk migrations in the fourth and fifth centuries CE, one of the more famous was the Vandals. Modern experts think their original homeland was situated in what is now northern Germany, close to the shores of the Baltic Sea. Around the start of the second century, they began moving southward and settled in modern-day Hungary.

For a few generations they appear to have been content to cause little more trouble than occasionally raiding the border areas of the nearby Roman provinces. Later, however, starting in the early fifth century, they joined with other Germanic tribes in crossing the Rhine River into Gaul (what is now France). No sooner had they begun settling there than other northern European tribal peoples challenged them for possession of the area.

The Vandals responded by migrating southward into Spain and then, in 429, into northwestern Africa. Next they marched eastward, swiftly overran the Roman-controlled lands in what is now Tunisia, and there founded a kingdom of their own. They did not remain idle for long. In 455 they sailed northward, boldly captured the city of Rome, looted it, and returned home. The Vandal kingdom lived on well after the Western Empire's government ceased to exist in 476. Only when the Eastern Roman emperor Justinian attacked and defeated the Vandals in the 530s did that fearsome Roman enemy disappear from the pages of history.

Diocletian initiated a series of sweeping reforms. The first consisted of converting the imperial government into a Persian-style monarchy in which the ruler was openly worshipped. He decreed that people had to address him as *dominus*, or "lord," and that all who approached him must bow and kiss his ring. He also added new layers of guards and spies in the imperial court, moves designed to discourage open dissent and assassination attempts.

In addition, Diocletian radically reformed the Empire's economy. Realizing that most coins had sunk in value to almost zero, he ordered his tax collectors to accept goods such as jewelry, food, and livestock as payment. The emperor also tried to regulate prices and wages in hopes of stopping prices from regularly going up.

Diocletian's most significant political reform was the largest overhaul of government leadership since Augustus had established the Empire. Administering such a huge collection of lands and peoples, Diocletian realized, was simply too hard for one person. So in a daring move, he split the realm in half. He took on the job of ruling the eastern half, choosing as his capital the city of Nicomedia, in northern Anatolia (what is now Turkey). To rule Rome's western sector, he appointed a strong military general, Maximian. A few years later, in 293, Diocletian further divided the ruling powers so that each half of the realm had a senior emperor and junior emperor. That four-man combination of imperial rulers came to be called the Tetrarchy.

> "In one of the most striking reversals in world history, Rome's foes were hurled back."[10]
>
> —Historian Michael Grant.

From Persecution to Powerhouse

Diocletian's reforms had the effect of breathing some new life into a badly ailing realm, so Rome's remarkable story continued. That emperor also inadvertently gave a fresh start to perhaps the most despised of Rome's religious groups. The Christians had initially appeared in the first century and had immediately been singled out for harassment. For various reasons, most people formed the mistaken impression that they were unbalanced, dangerous sociopaths who were intent on destroying the established order. So Christians became the objects of repeated persecutions. The unfairly abused Christians managed to hold on for more than two centuries. But in the year 300, at the height of Diocletian's reign, they still made up only 10 percent at best of the Empire's population.

Urged on by his coemperor Galerius, a rabid Christian hater, Diocletian launched the largest anti-Christian crusade yet. All across the realm's eastern sector, Christians were beaten, killed, and/or forced to watch the destruction of their holy writings and churches. However, this only inspired sympathy for them in the West. There, the two coemperors, Constantius and his son Constantine, had already befriended some Christians and refused to take part in the persecution.

Not long afterward, civil strife rocked both halves of the Empire, and Constantine eventually emerged the victor and sole ruler of the entire realm. He granted the Christians religious toleration and restored all the property they had lost in the recent persecution. This marked only the beginning of a series of enormous social and political gains for that long-vilified group. One of the more important ones was Constantine's establishment of a new Roman capital in the Empire's prosperous eastern region—Constantinople, near the entrance to the Black Sea. That so-called City of Constantine, founded in 330, was a Christian city from the outset, which served to legitimize and strengthen Christianity. Constantine also converted to Christianity on his deathbed in 337.

This and other boons to the growing Christian movement allowed it to permeate all levels of Roman society. Each of Constantine's sons was a committed Christian, as were all but one of the emperors who followed them. With the imperial court backing it, the faith prospered; by the 380s it had become a powerhouse and for all intents and purposes the Empire's official religion.

A Throat Laid Bare

Not all Romans converted to Christianity, however. Some remained pagans (ancient people who worshipped more than one god), in part because they did not like certain Christian beliefs and attitudes. Christians tended to be pacifists and discouraged people from becoming soldiers, for instance. To many pagans this seemed a suicidal stance to take in an increasingly dangerous world. In the 370s the Roman commonwealth had come under attack by waves of northern European tribes much larger than those of the preceding century. The era's pagans must have wondered, in Gibbon's words, "what must be the fate of the Empire, attacked on every side by the barbarians if all mankind should adopt the sentiments"[11] of the cowardly Christians?

The ongoing struggle between pagans and Christians and the fighting along the realm's northern borders proved to be only two of a number of serious problems that increasingly plagued Roman society. Another was a return to the unwise policy of dividing Rome's vast territories in half and thereby making each half weaker than the whole. When the emperor Theodosius died in 395, his sons, Arcadius and Honorius, each presided over half of a permanently divided realm.

Soldiers search for a Christian family in hiding. Beginning in the first century Christians were singled out for harassment and persecution, but by the late fourth century Christianity had essentially become the official religion of the Roman Empire.

As time went on, its separate spheres grew increasingly distant and distinct from each other.

Another grim reality was the diminishing power of Rome's once mighty military establishment. By the early years of the fifth century, the army had lost much of the discipline, mobility, and loyalty to the state that had been its proud hallmarks in prior centuries. The immediate effect of this military decline was to make stopping the growing tidal wave of foreign invaders more and more difficult.

Eventually, the relentless invasions, continuous loss of territory, economic problems, social and religious divisions among Romans, and poor leadership combined to take an awful toll in the West. The last few western emperors eventually oversaw a pathetic remnant of what had once been a great empire. The inevitable end, it turned out, was swift and surprisingly peaceful. In 476 a German-born Roman general named Odoacer decided to take advantage of an imperial government with its throat laid bare. He had his soldiers acclaim him king of Italy. Then he proceeded to an audience with the reigning emperor, an unassuming and clueless young man named Romulus Augustulus. Odoacer told him it was time for him to step down, and the emperor wisely did so.

Rome's Last Bastion

Because no official emperor took the boy-ruler's place, technically speaking the Western Empire no longer existed. Life went on as usual in Rome and other Italian towns for some time afterward. But each of the generations that followed saw itself as a little less Roman.

In the East, centered at Constantinople, meanwhile, the emperors and their subjects survived the catastrophe that had overwhelmed the West. The Eastern Roman realm, which modern historians came to call the Byzantine Empire, prospered for several centuries. But it, too, grew smaller and weaker over time, and it finally fell to the Ottoman Turks in 1453.

Right to the end, Constantinople's inhabitants thought of themselves as the last true Romans. Indeed, they referred to themselves the *Rhomaioi* (roh-MAY-ee), a Greek word meaning "Romans," and called their realm *Basileia Romaion*, the "Kingdom of the Romans." This strongly suggests that only *western* Rome perished in that often cited year, 476. In reality, the last bastion of old Rome fell fewer than six centuries ago. This means that if the cause of its demise—a massive siege by the Turks—had failed, the effects would surely have made the march of modern history very different. In that case the direct descendants of Caesar, Augustus, Marcus Aurelius, and Constantine might be ruling a realm called Rome today.

Did the Barbarian Invasions Cause Rome's Fall?

Focus Questions

1. How might history have been different if Rome's leaders had understood early on the true threat the northern European tribes posed to the Roman realm?
2. What was Julius Caesar's barbarian policy, and what would likely have happened if Rome had adopted it for all of Europe?
3. Why did the Roman defeat at Adrianople mark a turning point that led the Roman Empire into a downward political and military spiral?

"If people today know anything about the Roman Empire," states leading historian Adrian Goldsworthy, "it is that it fell. This is without doubt the best known 'fact' about ancient Rome."[12] Also, as Goldsworthy and other modern experts point out, that fact about Rome is a huge one. In the space of only about a century, the world's largest and most powerful empire—spanning much of Europe, plus most of Britain and large sectors of North Africa and the Middle East—had been utterly wiped off the map.

One Cause or Many?

One might think that an event of that tremendous size and importance would have an obvious, clear-cut cause that all could agree on. But that is not the case. Instead, as Goldsworthy himself says, "why Rome fell remains one of the great questions of history."[13] Indeed, hundreds of qualified modern historians have filled the pages of thousands of books and articles in earnest attempts to answer that question.

The first of these scholars, who is still seen as one of the finest, was Edward Gibbon in the late 1700s. His *Decline and Fall of the Roman Empire* remains *the* classic work of still-ongoing fall-of-Rome research and debates. The title of his "monumental work," Goldsworthy writes, "has become firmly imbedded in the wider consciousness. No other eighteenth-century history book has remained so regularly in print in various forms and editions until the present day." Indeed, says Goldsworthy, no other book on the subject "has ever challenged *The Decline and Fall of the Roman Empire*."[14]

One major reason that Gibbon's masterwork remains the gold standard of the genre is that he was an extraordinarily thorough and careful researcher. Also, he did not glibly try to isolate a single overarching cause for an effect as enormous as Rome's fall. Rather, he wisely saw that such a grandiose event must have had multiple causes. These, he insisted, had conspired to bring about the end of the old Roman world. As Michael Grant puts it, he listed "at least two dozen supposed causes of that decline and fall—military, political, economic, and psychological." Yet Gibbon "made no attempt to marshal them one against another, or choose between them. That is rather disconcerting to the reader who is searching for quick answers. But it also shows a good deal of prudence. For an enormous, complex institution like the Roman Empire could not have been obliterated by any single, simple cause."[15]

> "Why Rome fell remains one of the great questions of history."[13]
>
> —British historian Adrian Goldsworthy.

The Barbarian Attack Thesis

Using Gibbon's groundbreaking work as a sort of template, virtually all later historians accepted the multiple-cause thesis. It maintains that "the events of this period are tightly interwoven," as archaeologist Barry Cunliffe puts it. There were all sorts of social, economic, and military pressures "with which the decaying Roman state" was finally "unable to cope."[16]

Yet modern scholars have also offered complicated arguments suggesting that one, two, or three causes stood out as the major culprits behind Rome's fall. Of these, perhaps the most often-cited theory is that the key cause of Rome's ultimate ruin was military in nature.

More specifically, that argument states, the Empire's borders were battered by northern European peoples—the so-called barbarians—over the course of several centuries. These attacks in a sense wore down the realm in a cumulative way over time. This was especially the case, the theory's proponents say, in Rome's last century, when the barbarian assaults became truly colossal in their size and the negative effects they brought about.

No scholar has summed up this particular example of cause and effect better than Gibbon himself. "The Romans were ignorant of the extent of their danger, and the number of their enemies," he wrote. "Beyond the Rhine and Danube [Rivers], the northern countries of Europe and Asia were filled with innumerable tribes of hunters and shepherds" who were poor, in turmoil, and greedy for land. They were "bold in arms, and impatient to ravish the fruits of industry," Gibbon went on. "The barbarian world was agitated by the rapid impulse of war." These restless tribes had been seized by "the spirit of conquest. The endless column of barbarians pressed on the Roman Empire with accumulated weight, and if the foremost were destroyed, the vacant space was instantly replenished by new assailants."[17] In this way the barbarians steadily wore down the Romans until resistance was ultimately futile. The Empire was condemned to permanent defeat and obliteration.

> "The barbarian world was agitated by the rapid impulse of war."[17]
>
> —Eighteenth-century British historian Edward Gibbon.

No scholar of ancient times doubts that what Gibbon here described happened (along with social and other causes for Rome's fall). The question those experts often ask is whether this series of military incidents by itself made Rome's demise inevitable. That is, would that awful outcome have definitely occurred once the barbarian migrations and attacks had gotten under way?

Choosing Defense over Offense

The answer that some historians give to this question is a resounding no. Rome was *not* necessarily doomed by the onrush of the barbarians, they say, in part because the assaults by those peoples took place over a long time span. Indeed, the tribes within the Germanic and Celtic

Barbarians bring death and destruction to Rome. Barbarian attacks from Europe's northern regions steadily and relentlessly destroyed the Empire's defenses, resulting eventually in absolute defeat.

civilizations that inhabited northern Europe in those days launched incursions into Roman lands on and off for several centuries. Moreover, according to this view, had the Romans dealt with these attackers in a decisive manner earlier, the massive invasions of the fifth century may not have happened. Or at least they would have been far smaller, and as a result Rome might well have survived.

Attila's Legendary Reputation

The Huns, a fierce, nomadic Asian people who appeared on the scene in the 370s, terrorized the northern European tribes as much as they did the Romans. In the 430s a new Hunnic leader, Attila, arose and subsequently launched attacks on both Eastern and Western Roman towns and cities. Jennifer Laing, an expert on early barbarian Europe, here suggests that Attila's enormous reputation for both savagery and heroics may have been somewhat inflated.

> The new Hunnic leader was described as a lover of war, though personally restrained in action. He was impressive in counsel, gracious to those asking help, and generous with those he trusted. He was snub-nosed, short, swarthy, and broad-chested with a massive head, small eyes, and a thin, grey-sprinkled beard. Few could argue with [sixth-century Roman politician] Jordanes' opinion that Attila was born to "shake the peoples of the world." Yet few people, if any, have been the subject of more distortion and more legend. While he was undoubtedly the leader of some very aggressive and persistent groups, there seems little justification for hailing him as either a genius or a hero. His reputation in popular lore has been exaggerated to an unfounded degree, though he was certainly charismatic. The least that can be said is that he was born at the right time, in the right place, and with the right personal attributes to achieve more than the average in an unusually spectacular manner.

Jennifer Laing, *Warriors of the Dark Ages.* Gloucestershire: Sutton, 2000, pp. 38–39.

An examination of what actually occurred seems to support this view. First, when various European peoples assailed Rome's northern provinces in the late Republic and early Empire, the Romans stopped their advances. Yet they usually opted not to follow up with major offensive campaigns into those peoples' homelands. Rather, with one notable exception, the Empire was always on the *defensive* and failed to take advantage of obvious opportunities to severely weaken the barbarian tribes. This allowed the barbarians' numbers, power, and boldness to greatly increase, almost ensuring their ultimate success.

A clear example of this hesitant approach to dealing with the northern tribes took place in the late second century BCE. By that time, the Roman Republic was a powerful realm that controlled most of Italy, along with a majority of the lands directly bordering the Mediterranean Sea. Between 109 and 106 BCE, two large Germanic tribes—the Cimbri and Teutones—moved into northern Italy after defeating several small Roman forces that had been sent to stop them. Fear rippled through the towns and cities of the Roman commonwealth.

Fortunately for the Roman people, in that hour of their need Rome's greatest living military general, Gaius Marius, rode north at the head of his army and crushed the intruders. In this case what Marius did was of less consequence in the long run than what he did *not* do. He and his fellow Roman generals had enough soldiers and resources to carry that brief war northward to the enemy's homeland. The largest, most dangerous Germanic forces that then existed had just been thoroughly defeated. So the Romans almost certainly could have overrun and captured the territories lying just north of Italy. Those lands would then have become a Roman-controlled buffer zone that would have made that part of the realm safer for generations to come.

Caesar's Barbarian Policy

For reasons that are unclear, however, Roman leaders did not feel that such a major offensive campaign was necessary. Evidently, they assumed that the Cimbri's and Teutones' invasion was an isolated threat that Marius had decisively dealt with. At the time, the Roman government did not seem to foresee that the northern tribes might become a much larger threat in the future.

However, not every Roman notable proved as shortsighted. Marius's own nephew (by marriage), Julius Caesar, was one of the few major leaders in Rome's final five centuries who saw the wisdom of going on the offensive in the north. It remains unknown whether Caesar desired or planned to bring the rest of Europe into the Roman fold. Considering what happened later, in the fourth and fifth centuries, that would clearly have been a smart move for the Rome of his day. If the northern barbarians had been absorbed and Romanized at that time, the immense invasions of those later centuries likely would not have occurred.

Whatever Caesar's ultimate plans may have been, he did invade Gaul (now France, Netherlands, and Belgium). Starting in 58 BCE, he led one military campaign after another against the mostly Celtic

During Julius Caesar's invasion of Gaul, Roman forces overtake the Gallic stronghold of Bourges. Although it was initially spared, Caesar's forces later destroyed the city and killed most of its inhabitants.

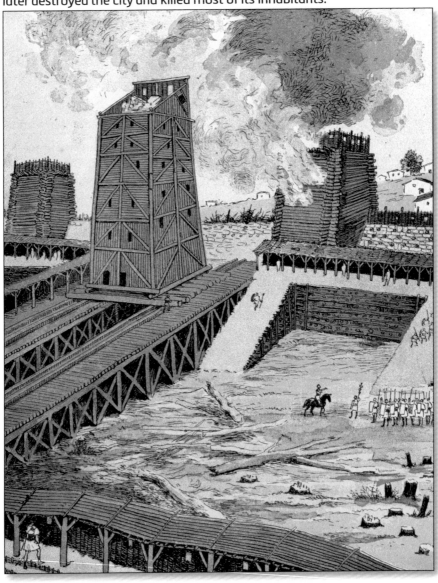

tribes that then resided in that region. A mere eight years later, most of Gaul was pacified, and in the century that followed the once fierce and independent tribesmen were converted into prosperous, productive, and loyal Romans.

Clearly, Caesar had proved the wisdom of going on the offensive and incorporating barbarian Europe into the Roman commonwealth. But would future Roman leaders follow his example? For a while, it appeared that his most important immediate successor, his adopted son, Octavian, would do just that.

Augustus and the Barbarians

After emerging the victor of the civil wars that brought down the Roman Republic, Octavian, renamed Augustus, initially planned to meet the issue of the northern Germanic tribes head on. He saw that some of those groups lived only 200 miles (322 km) north of Italy. In his mind, having the barbarians so close to the Roman heartland was risky at best. So he developed a strategy that would extend the northern borders by some 150 miles (241 km), bringing them up to the Danube River. At his order, Roman armies slowly but steadily moved into German lands. These efforts were not only successful but also largely peaceful, and by 15 BCE four new provinces had been created in the region just south of the Danube.

This northern frontier did not stay calm for long, however. Small groups of Germans started raiding the new Roman provinces. In response, Augustus sent soldiers northward, past the Danube and into the region bordered by the Rhine, Danube, and Elbe Rivers. His generals also began trying to Romanize the local natives in the same way that Rome was already converting the peoples of Gaul.

One of the chief figures in this ongoing cultural conversion process was a general named Publius Quinctilius Varus. Augustus sent him to negotiate with German leaders and to pave the way for the establishment of still another new province. There was a serious problem, however. Varus was an incredibly arrogant and insensitive individual who proceeded to alienate the people he was supposed to Romanize. Feeling insulted and threatened, in 9 CE the Germans secretly assembled a large force of warriors and attacked him and his troops in the Teutoburg Forest, roughly 80 miles (129 km) east of the Rhine. Varus and his three legions—totaling about fifteen thousand soldiers—were slaughtered.

Augustus took the news of the calamity badly. Normally not given to outward displays of emotion, he "left his hair and beard untrimmed for months," wrote the first-century-CE Roman historian Suetonius. Also, "he would often beat his head on a door, shouting: 'Quinctilius Varus, give me back my legions!'"[18]

Varus could not give the legions back, of course. Furthermore, properly replacing those men and their gear and weapons would have nearly bankrupted Augustus. So he became disheartened and pulled the rest of Rome's forces out of central Europe, thereby returning the area to the Germans.

Even worse, the first emperor's immediate successors followed his example. As the Romanized Greek historian Appian observed a bit more than a century later, "Possessing the best part of the earth and sea," the Romans "have, on the whole, aimed to preserve their empire by the exercise of prudence, rather than to extend their sway indefinitely over poverty-stricken and profitless tribes of barbarians." Those tribes nevertheless remained a potent threat, Appian pointed out. "They surround the empire with great armies," he said, "and they garrison [station military forces in] the whole stretch of land and sea like a single stronghold."[19]

> "[The barbarian tribes] surround the empire with great armies and they garrison the whole stretch of land and sea like a single stronghold."[19]
>
> —Second-century-CE Greek historian Appian.

From Victory to Humiliating Defeat

Appian had good reason to be concerned about the potential threat the northern European tribes posed to the Empire. With each passing decade the German lands became more populous and in some areas more restless. One perilous result of this trend occurred in 166 when the Marcommani and some other Germanic tribes assaulted the northern borders. With great difficulty, the last of the so-called good emperors, Marcus Aurelius, drove these assailants back.

One of the shrewdest of Rome's long line of national leaders, Aurelius seems to have considered moving into and Romanizing the in-

Ammianus on the Rout at Adrianople

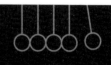

The fourth-century Roman historian Ammianus Marcellinus, who was about fifty at the time of the slaughter at Adrianople, composed an account of the battle that has survived. It says in part:

> Amid the clashing of arms and weapons on every side, while Bellona [the Roman war goddess], raging with more than her usual fury, was sounding the death-knell of the Roman cause, our retreating troops rallied with shouts of mutual encouragement. But, as the fighting spread like fire and numbers of them were transfixed by arrows and whirling javelins, they lost heart. Then the opposing lines came into collision like ships of war and pushed each other to and fro, heaving under the reciprocal motion like the waves of the sea. Our left wing penetrated as far as the very wagons [holding the Goths' women and children], and would have gone further if it had received any support, but it was abandoned by the rest of the cavalry, and under pressure of numbers gave way and collapsed like a broken dyke. This left the infantry unprotected and so closely huddled together that a man could hardly wield his sword or draw back his arm once he had stretched it out. Dust rose in such clouds as to hide the sky, which rang with frightful shouts. . . . The barbarians poured on in huge columns, trampling down horse and man and crushing our ranks so as to make an orderly retreat impossible.

Ammianus Marcellinus, *History,* published as *The Later Roman Empire, A.D. 354–378,* trans. and ed. Walter Hamilton. New York: Penguin, 1986, p. 435.

vaders' homelands. That plan never came to pass, however. Aurelius passed away in 180, and his irresponsible son, Commodus, ascended the throne. Commodus in essence bribed the German tribes to stay on their side of the border, which more or less maintained the status quo.

Largely left to their own devices by the series of mostly inept Roman rulers that followed, those tribes once more burst out of their home territories in the 230s. Soon the crisis that many modern scholars call the Anarchy was in full swing. In 251 one of the strongest of the Germanic groups, the Goths, entered the fray and defeated and slew the emperor Decius. After dividing into two main factions—the Visigoths and Ostrogoths—they greatly encouraged other tribes to challenge Rome. Among these were the Alamanni, who made it all the way into northern Italy before a Roman army stopped them.

Somehow the Romans managed to hold on and survive the Anarchy, in part because the last few soldier-emperors, especially Diocletian (ruled 284–305), were strong leaders. As a result, during his reign and those of his immediate successors, the northern borders remained reasonably quiet. But sure enough, the Romans again grew complacent, mistakenly thinking the danger from the north was more or less over. In the first decades of the fourth century, the Germanic tribes continued to grow in numbers. Unbeknownst to Rome's leaders, moreover, the likelihood that the Visigoths and others would once more march southward steadily increased.

It turned out to be an unexpected landmark event that set those now inevitable invasions in motion. In 370 a hostile people from central Asia—the Huns—pushed their way into eastern Europe. Described by the fourth-century Roman historian Ammianus Marcellinus as "quite abnormally savage,"[20] the Huns rapidly annihilated the kingdom the Ostrogoths had recently created in what is now Ukraine. In turn, some two hundred thousand petrified Visigoths fled across the Danube into Roman territory.

Hardly less afraid himself, the emperor Valens (reigned 364–378) tried to strike a deal with the Visigoths in which they would settle on Roman lands in exchange for contributing soldiers to the Roman army. But his agents stupidly tried to exploit the newcomers, who responded violently. In an even more unwise move, the pigheaded Valens then attacked the Visigoths in August 378. At Adrianople (then in northern Greece, now in northwestern Turkey), the emperor and roughly forty thousand of his men fell in a humiliating, historic defeat.

Attila, leader of the Huns, points to a large and wealthy Roman city that his troops will shortly conquer. The Huns made their way across Europe from Asia, decimating whole kingdoms as they went.

Back into the Italian Soil

At the time, all Romans acknowledged that the awful losses at Adrianople constituted a crippling defeat. What they could not foresee was that this critical event foreshadowed the Empire's eventual slide into nonexistence. One of the many aspects of this fateful decline was Rome's inability to restore all the soldiers and equipment lost at Adrianople. That terrible rout also did significant psychological damage, as thereafter the Roman people became increasingly anxious about the future.

This negative attitude only worsened. In the last years of the fourth century and the first few decades of the fifth, Europe was engulfed in military and social upheavals the like of which it had never before experienced. Numerous Celtic and Germanic groups roamed across the continent in search of new homes. "The picture," Cunliffe explains, "is one of roving bands of men, women, and children forced out of their homelands, spreading south and west into the crumbling Roman Empire." He adds, "Sometimes they were in conflict with the remnant Roman armies," while other times "they worked with them to oppose further incursions."[21]

In desperation, several Roman emperors tried to bargain with the intruders. Often the latter were allowed to settle down permanently in Roman territory as long as they became allies and supplied soldiers for the fast-weakening Roman army. Many such deals were struck. But usually the lands on which those barbarians settled were no longer under direct Roman authority. The result was that Rome steadily lost control of enormous sections of its former provinces. As the 400s wore on, therefore, the Western Roman realm swiftly disintegrated.

Indeed, "the situation fast became impossible," Cunliffe writes. "Gradually the western part of the Empire took on a new appearance as the old order became submerged beneath the tide of newcomers."[22] The barbarians' *accumulated weight*, in Gibbon's immortal words, had in a symbolic sense driven one of history's greatest realms back into the Italian soil that had nourished the earliest Romans.

Did Internal Disunities Fatally Weaken Rome?

Focus Questions

1. What were the succeeding stages of the Empire's physical division, and how did these affect Rome's ability to defend itself from attack?
2. How did members of Rome's lower classes react to being exploited by government leaders and other upper-class individuals in the fourth and fifth centuries?
3. How did the rise of Christianity in the fourth century gradually erode Rome's traditional martial spirit?

In addition to the onrush of the barbarian tribes from outside the Empire, certain internal factors contributed to Rome's decline and ultimate fall. Historians often refer to many of these factors as disunities or disharmonies. By themselves, these internal disunities would likely not have doomed Rome. It was the combination of these troubles, compounded by the barbarian invasions, that was ruinous in the end. As one historian argues: "In accumulation, they proved fatal. By making resistance to the external onslaughts impossible, they swept the western Roman Empire out of existence."[23]

Some of those internal problems were clearly political in nature. The division of the Empire into two distinct geographical sections, for example, caused two separate Roman realms to develop. As the two steadily grew apart, each came to be primarily concerned with its own security and personal dilemmas. So when western Rome was in serious trouble and needed extra manpower and other resources to meet the threat of the barbarian incursions, the Eastern Empire offered little help.

There were also social and religious disunities. For instance, the wealthy classes—whose members controlled the government—frequently exploited the poor. At the same time, both the poor and the rich often resented the government and attempted to subvert the laws it tried to enforce. Meanwhile, as Christianity gained strength in the fourth century, its members regularly clashed with pagans. In a reversal of the earlier tendency for pagans to persecute Christians, pagans sometimes found themselves the objects of discrimination.

A Capital to Rival Rome

Certainly the most visual political disunity that developed in Rome's final few centuries was the division of the Empire into western and eastern sectors. Most Romans did not perceive the danger this process posed to the western realm's security until it was too late, and that was because it happened so gradually. It started in a subtle way toward the end of the third century. Carinus and Numerian, brothers who ruled the Empire jointly from 283 to 284, sought to make the military easier to manage by splitting its operations into eastern and western zones.

The brothers' immediate successor, Diocletian, then built upon this idea in the political reforms that ultimately resulted in the division of rule known as the Tetrarchy. He and his junior emperor ruled the East from the city of Nicomedia and an appointed team of senior and junior emperors ruled the West. At this point, the Empire was not yet physically divided. Diocletian remained the most powerful tetrarch, and behind the scenes he retained control of the whole realm. Also, the age-old city of Rome, located in the West, easily overshadowed the newer and much smaller Nicomedia in the East.

> "[A] multitude of laborers and artists urged the conclusion of the work with incessant toil."[24]
>
> —Eighteenth-century British historian Edward Gibbon on the building of Constantinople.

However, this situation was significantly altered after Constantine erected his impressive new Christian city, Constantinople, in 330. One of his intentions in this endeavor was to create an imposing new eastern capital that would outshine Rome, and he succeeded. No one had ever before attempted to build a city to rival Rome, and to do so required enormous resources of money and manpower. To create this "eternal monument of the glories of his reign," Edward Gibbon said, Constantine exploited "the wealth, the labor, and all that yet remained of the genius of obedient millions." A virtual "multitude of laborers and artists urged the conclusion of the work with incessant toil."[24]

The eastern capital of Christendom, Constantinople, outshone Rome. The emperor Constantine I devoted enormous resources of money and manpower to its creation.

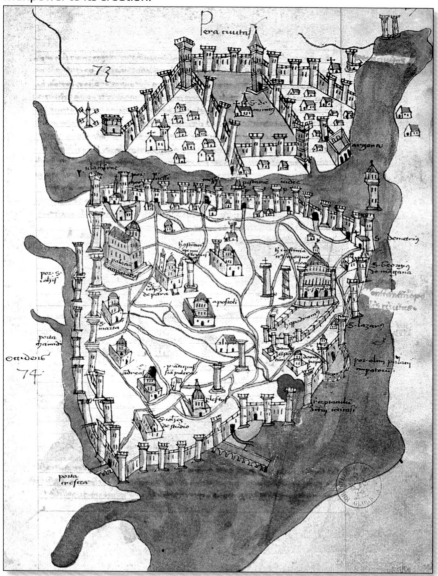

Toward a Two-Part Empire

Once the Empire had two equally resplendent capital cities, another crucial step in the realm's division occurred in 364. Sitting on the imperial throne in Rome, the emperor Valentinian I began his rule of the realm's western sector. He also appointed his brother, Valens, as coemperor, giving him almost complete control over the Empire's eastern half. The two rulers proceeded to divide up almost everything of importance, including military officers and courtiers.

The result was two separate imperial courts of equal splendor, each administering its own distinct Roman region. Nevertheless, technically speaking those regions were not completely separate, because Valentinian wisely retained seniority, just as Diocletian had within the Tetrarchy. So Valentinian was able to overrule Valens if necessity dictated it.

The division of the realm into two separate imperial units of equal authority took place toward the end of the fourth century, following the death of Theodosius. He was the last emperor to exert sole rule over both the Eastern and Western Roman regions. Yet he saw that their separation was inevitable, and he crafted a succession plan for his two sons to follow after his death. That historic event occurred in 395. Guided by imperial advisors, the sons—Honorius, aged eleven, and Arcadius, aged seventeen—each took charge of his half of the Empire. Honorius reigned in the West and Arcadius oversaw the East. From that time on, Rome had not only two capitals, but also two distinct national policies, making it a *partes imperii*, a Latin term meaning "two-part Empire."

On paper, so to speak, this did not seem like a bad idea. But in practice, it turned out to be a mistake that negatively affected both realms. The most immediate problem was that their treasuries and military resources were separate, which made each financially and militarily weaker than it had been as part of a single, larger realm. This especially hurt the western realm. "The western provinces were much more exposed to barbarian attack,"[25] the late, great historian A.H.M. Jones pointed out.

The Rich Against the Poor

The partition of the Empire into two sectors, each weaker than the original, proved to be only one of many disunities that ate away at

Ammianus Marcellinus was a fourth-century Greek-speaking Roman who composed a massive history book, parts of which survive. A thorough, clear, and fair historian, he sometimes ridiculed the arrogant wealthy individuals who thought themselves superior to the poor people they exploited. At one point in his narrative, he says of those conceited rich that they

> think that the height of glory is to be found in unusually high carriages and an ostentatious style of dress. They sweat under the burden of cloaks which they attach to their necks and fasten at the throat. These being of very fine texture, are easily blown about, and they *contrive* by frequent movements, especially of the left hand, to show off their long fringes and display the garments beneath, which are embroidered with various animal fringes. Others again, with an appearance of deep gravity, hold forth [speak] unasked on the immense extent of their family property, multiplying in imagination the annual produce of their fertile lands, which extend, they boastfully declare, from farthest east to farthest west.... Some, regardless of the risk, gallop their horses at the speed of the public post through open spaces and paved streets of the city, hell [bent] for leather, as the phrase goes. Behind them come their slaves in crowds like a gang of highwaymen.

Ammianus Marcellinus, *History*, published as *The Later Roman Empire, A.D. 354–378*, trans. and ed. Walter Hamilton. New York: Penguin, 1986, pp. 46–48.

Rome's fabric. A steady deterioration of relations between rich and poor Romans was another. For instance, in the West—the main target of the barbarian invaders—taxes levied on the poor by the government, run by members of the wealthy class, were often brutal.

Crushing the lower classes under excessive taxation was nothing new. It had been a common practice in many ancient societies, including that of Rome in some of its prior ages. But this time it brought about a fatal disunity. Filled with resentment, at times even rage, some poor Roman farmers, laborers, and artisans went so far as to abandon their homes in order to escape tax collectors. Some of these homeless poor banded together for mutual protection. They formed *bagaudae*, nomadic groups of peasants who survived any way they could and fought back against any soldiers the government sent to arrest or eradicate them.

Often both *bagaudae* and single families or individuals resettled in regions where Roman tax collectors could not reach them. This included areas recently captured by various barbarian groups. "What else can these wretched people wish for?" asked a Roman Christian named Salvian. In his writings, he described the plight of impoverished Roman settlers in Gaul in the mid-400s. They suffered "the incessant and even continuous destruction of public tax levies," he said. "To them there is always imminent a heavy and relentless proscription," or government effort to find, punish, and tax them. The barbarians are "more lenient to them than the tax collectors." Indeed, resettled Romans pray "that they be allowed to carry on the life they lead with the barbarians."[26]

> "The taxes which were needed to pay for the army could not be raised. And because they could not be raised, the Empire failed to find defenders, and collapsed."[27]
>
> —Historian Michael Grant.

In this and similar ways, upper-class government officials oppressed the poorest Romans, causing a steady decrease in their loyalty to Rome. "The state and the underprivileged bulk of its rural subjects were set against each other in a destructive and suicidal disharmony," Michael Grant writes. This serious problem "played a very large and direct part in the downfall that followed. It was because of this rift that the taxes which were needed to pay for the army could not be raised. And because they could not be raised, the Empire failed to find defenders, and collapsed."[27]

The Rich Against the Rich

Just as many of Rome's poorer individuals lost respect for the government and upper classes, so too did numerous elements of those classes come to feel it was *they* who were mistreated. Most wealthy Romans were hugely arrogant. They looked on the common folk as social inferiors and felt a strong sense of entitlement. That is, they believed that both the government and the poor owed them an easy ride in life. The fair-minded Ammianus saw it very differently. Putting them in their place, he quipped, "they presumably do not know that their ancestors, who were responsible for the expansion of Rome, did not owe their distinction to riches, but overcame all obstacles by their valor."[28]

One of the several ways the wealthiest Romans felt misused involved the large amounts of money the government had come to expect from them. Not only did they pay high taxes, they also supported the gladiatorial combats, chariot races, and other popular public games. For centuries, the government had borne the chief burden of those entertainments. From the late fourth century on, however, the state was often on the verge of bankruptcy. So it increasingly called upon, and eventually forced, the richest citizens to empty their own pockets to pay for the public games.

The victor of a gladiatorial combat looks to spectators for how to deal with his defeated adversary. Wealthy Romans avidly supported such games but resented having to pay for them when government funds dwindled.

The rich also resented the fact that the government's frequent lack of funds had caused most cities and towns to fall increasingly into disrepair. Since the days of the Republic, large numbers of wealthy landowners had been absentee landlords—urban dwellers who paid people to manage their large country estates. But as the cities became dirtier, less comfortable places to live, those landowners started withdrawing to those rural estates. There, the late scholar Harold Mattingly wrote, "they might defy the tax collector, harbor refugees from justice, and in general comport themselves as little lords."[29] Indeed, the biggest of these estates "were whole little kingdoms unto themselves," in Grant's

Turning the Tables on the Pagans

As Christianity steadily rose to social and political prominence in the fourth century, its leaders increasingly launched verbal attacks on Roman paganism. In addition, in the final decades of that century some Christians spit on and/or vandalized pagan shrines and temples across the Empire. Meanwhile, a number of Christian bishops ardently condemned pagan beliefs and worship. By far the most prominent of these zealous bishops was Ambrose of Milan (ca. 340–397), who knew and heavily influenced several Roman emperors. Ambrose argued that Christianity was the only true faith and that pagan worship should be neither respected nor tolerated.

Hoping to strike a major blow against the pagans, he convinced the western emperor Gratian (ruled 367–383) to give up a traditional post held by all emperors up to that point—high priest of Rome's state religion. Ambrose also persuaded Gratian to cancel state financial support for pagan priests and to remove the statue of the goddess Victory from Rome's Senate House. Leading pagans were shocked at such disrespect for long-established religious traditions. They pleaded with the emperor to restore the statue and halt further sacrilege, but such appeals fell on deaf ears. Some of the more tolerant Christians also implored their leaders to be more respectful. But they were outnumbered by those who held that, since pagans had once persecuted Christians, turning the tables on the former persecutors was perfectly justified.

words. The owners surrounded themselves with small armies of armed guards and their homes "were fortified like castles."[30]

In these and similar ways, many rich landowners came to oppose the equally wealthy rulers. Those landowners not only distanced themselves from the central government, they also socially mingled with the leading Celtic and Germanic tribesmen who became their neighbors in rural regions. So when the government ceased to function in 476, these former Roman nobles made an easy transition. They simply switched allegiance and joined the upper classes of the Germanic kingdoms that grew upon the Empire's wreckage. In this way much of the old Roman aristocracy managed to survive western Rome's demise.

The Christians Too Divisive?

Even as these political and social forces were reshaping Rome's declining culture, so too were religious events and pressures. In particular, the realm's deeply rooted and long-respected pagan faith was giving way to the swiftly expanding ranks of Christians. Gibbon was the first modern historian to propose that Christianity played an important role in western Rome's fall. He held that that faith fatally weakened Roman society in various ways.

Gibbon was not anti-Christian; in fact, he was a devout follower of the faith. Like later scholars of Roman civilization, he examined the effects of Christianity on Rome in a detached manner and refrained from judging either that religion or the pagan faiths that preceded it. Gibbon simply made the point that many Christian beliefs and values were inconsistent with pagan ones. At the time, he argued, the decline of traditional Roman religious beliefs and institutions in favor of Christian ones made the Empire less able to defend itself against the encroaching barbarians.

One reason for this, according to Gibbon and most other historians, was that during the fourth and fifth centuries the Christians tended to be more divisive than the pagans. More specifically, most Christians of that era refused to respect the tenets of other faiths. This attitude was rooted in strong feelings of religious exclusivity, as they believed their god was the only one in existence. In contrast, the religiously tolerant Romans saw this position as narrow-minded. They accepted the then prevailing view—that there were diverse paths to the same heavenly truths, and therefore everyone's gods were real and worthy of respect. In part because the Christians rejected this idea, the Romans came to see them as fanatics and troublemakers. "The main charge against the Christians," Jones wrote, "was that they were atheists who denied and insulted all the gods."[31]

Another way the Christians were divisive in the Empire's final century was that their leaders encouraged people to drop out of so-

Christians bury their dead in Rome's underground catacombs. Christians of the era were much less tolerant of other faiths than the Romans, who came to see the Christians as fanatics and troublemakers.

ciety. This marked the genesis of the monastic movement (from the Greek word *monachos*, meaning "solitary"), in which devout individuals gave up their regular lives and became monks, nuns, and other religious recluses. Most Christians believed the monastic movement was healthy. It was a thoughtful way for people to express their deep love for God, they argued. Most pagan leaders countered that the mounting numbers of religious dropouts drained society of valuable human resources at a time when Rome was fighting for its very existence.

> "The main charge against the Christians was that they were atheists who denied and insulted all the gods."[31]
>
> —Classics scholar A.H.M. Jones.

Escaping the Draft

Still another reason that Christianity caused disunity in that fateful era, many scholars contend, is that its beliefs were too pacifistic. In clearly dangerous times, when the Empire badly needed soldiers to fight the barbarians, leading Christians urged men not to become soldiers. The bishops refused to accept "that it was lawful on any occasion to shed the blood of [their] fellow-creatures," Gibbon explained, "either by the sword of justice, or by that of war."[32]

Some pagan Romans accepted this ultra-pacifistic concept and joined the Christian ranks. Others converted simply to have an excuse to avoid serving in the army. Either way, this had the effect of weakening Rome's old and venerable martial spirit and making it increasingly difficult to raise new military recruits.

When the government became desperate for those recruits, it forced many young men into service. Some sliced off their own thumbs in hopes of escaping the military draft, but the army took them anyway. These men often ended up in the front lines of battle, facing onrushing masses of screaming barbarians. But this new brand of Roman soldier was a far cry from those who had valiantly pushed the realm's borders ever outward in prior ages. In the darker days of the fifth century, it was not unusual for young soldiers, Christian and non-Christian alike, to drop their weapons and run away. That spelled almost certain disaster. When traditional Roman patriotism began to fade, the Empire's days were clearly numbered.

Did Economic and Military Factors Destroy Rome?

Focus Questions

1. What were the immediate and long-term effects of Roman peasants abandoning their farms during the third, fourth, and fifth centuries?
2. In what ways do Diocletian's economic reforms parallel or differ from economic strategies in modern society? How successful were his efforts?
3. How did Rome's major military strategy change in the Empire's last two centuries, and why did that change not help protect the realm from the invading barbarian tribes?

One of the Roman Empire's key strengths during its successful first two centuries was its vibrant economy. Agriculture and trade flourished, and overall taxes were low. (The residents of Italy, the traditional Roman heartland, paid no direct taxes at all until the late 200s.) As a result, the imperial treasury was full enough to support lavish public entertainments and extensive building projects across the realm. Enormous public baths arose. Those who attended, rich and poor alike, could relax, have a massage, exercise, enjoy a snack, or read a book—all for a minimal fee and as often as desired. With few exceptions, Romans were happy and looked forward to what seemed like a limitless future of relative peace and prosperity.

During the third century, however, the Empire's economy suffered one devastating hit after another. Society felt the damaging effects of almost continual warfare, a rise in lawlessness, agricultural decline, and reduced long-range trade. There was also a devaluation of common coins, which in some cases became nearly worthless.

Trying to make up for the economic shortfall, the government sharply raised taxes on those who already paid them and eventually introduced taxes to those who had been exempt. It did not take long, therefore, for general feelings of misery to replace the sense of contentment and security that had prevailed only a few years before. The economy improved a bit in the first decades of the fourth century. But soon the onset of the barbarian invasions caused it to decline again. After that, more and more Romans found it increasingly difficult to make ends meet.

The economic downward spiral was accompanied by a fatal downturn in the quality of the once powerful Roman military system. Among the causes of the army's decline were poor leadership, misguided strategic decisions in trying to halt the barbarian incursions, and increased difficulty in finding eligible, effective new recruits. Many modern scholars agree with historian Arther Ferrill's thesis that the deterioration of the imperial army was as crucial as the barbarian invasions themselves in causing western Rome's fall. "At the opening of the fifth century," he writes, "a massive army, perhaps more than 200,000 strong, stood at the service of the western emperor and his generals. In 476 it was gone. The destruction of Roman military power in the fifth century" was a major cause "of the collapse of the Roman government in the West."[33]

> "At the opening of the fifth century, a massive army, perhaps more than 200,000 strong, stood at the service of the western emperor and his generals. In 476 it was gone."[33]
>
> —Military historian Arther Ferrill.

An Awful Drain of Funds

The decline of both the economy and army were horribly dire events that the Romans of the prosperous second century CE could not in their wildest imaginations have foreseen. As Ferrill points out, they enjoyed "a basic standard of living that remains a marvel in the history of Western civilization."[34]

The rise of immense public bathhouses is symbolic of the overall Roman achievement. The Romans of that period were physically cleaner than most other ancient peoples. In addition, those grand bathing facilities, along with public fountains within reach of all urban

Romans, had access to enormous amounts of fresh water. It was "often transported hundreds of miles in the famous systems of aqueducts,"[35] Ferrill writes. Those bountiful water supplies also made agriculture a success, so there was always plenty to eat. Likewise, the well-heeled government provided the public shows and a system of fair laws and prompt justice, and all these aspects of civilized life were safeguarded by the strongest army the world had yet seen.

The first sign of weakness in the muscular economic framework that supported that exceptional standard of living occurred shortly after Marcus Aurelius's death in 180. His self-absorbed son, Commodus, frequently used monies from the public treasury on wasteful personal projects and luxuries. This in itself was trivial compared to the size and

Rome's famous baths attracted rich and poor alike. For a minimal fee, Rome's inhabitants could relax, enjoy a massage, snack, and exercise at the public baths.

outlay of the overall imperial economy. Yet in retrospect, it foreshadowed the awful drain on public and private funds to come.

Sure enough, following Commodus's assassination in 192, decades of political uncertainty, civil wars, and foreign invasions set in. To finance their expensive military campaigns, the emperors and their governors sharply raised taxes. In turn, many people who were by today's standards middle class fell into poverty, and those who had already been poor became destitute. Farming and trade suffered. Meanwhile, to help counteract the shrinking treasury, the imperial mints stopped using gold and silver for coins and replaced those metals with cheaper alloys. That caused those coins to drop in value. So as time went on, more and more people were able to buy less and less.

The economy grew even worse as trade was frequently disrupted altogether. Pirates and other thieves robbed farmers and travelers alike. In addition, military generals often could not afford to pay their soldiers, some of whom got what was owed them by looting the farms and villages of their own countrymen.

During the late third century, therefore, and on into Rome's final two centuries, it was common for poor peasants to abandon their farms. Large tracts of those once fertile lands became overgrown with weeds or dried out, eroded, and became worthless. An anonymous document from the early fourth century describes a region in Gaul where many acres of productive land had reverted to nature. "Whatever usable soil there was has been ruined by swamps and choked with briers," it says in part. The once fruitful farmlands of the district lie mostly "uncultivated, neglected, silent, shadowy."[36]

Halfway Between Freedom and Slavery

While this was happening, the peasants who had left those lands hardly knew where to turn. Some moved to the cities. There a few found occasional work as laborers, but many became beggars or lived off whatever small amount of free bread the government could afford to hand out. The rest of the landless poor became tenant farmers who worked small plots of soil on vast estates owned by a few wealthy lords. Most of these tenant farmers grew financially dependent on those rich landlords and could not afford to move or set up their own farms or businesses. These dependent farmworkers became known as *coloni*. In the words of historian Arthur Boak:

> Their condition was halfway between that of free men and that of slaves. While they were bound to the estates upon which they resided and passed with it from one owner to another, they were not absolutely under the power of the owner and could not be disposed of [sold] by him apart from the land. They had also other rights which slaves lacked, yet as time went on their condition tended to approximate more and more to servitude more and more closely. "Slaves of the soil" they were called.[37]

At various times in the fourth century, the abuse of the *coloni* became permanently entrenched via a series of laws. One said, "It will be proper for such [*coloni*] as contemplate flight to be bound with chains to a servile status, so that by virtue of such condemnation to servitude they may be compelled to fulfill the duties that befit free men."[38]

Other Economic Problems

While increasing numbers of penniless Romans were forced into servitude, many others who were at least somewhat solvent faced different sorts of financial problems. Some fell deeply into debt and never managed to climb back out. One common way that such debts accumulated was that prices constantly went up, while the amount people earned stayed the same or even went down. As a result, many people borrowed money just to make ends meet. But as prices of necessary goods continued to rise, there simply was no way to get ahead and pay back the loans. In turn, the overall standard of living decreased and poverty increased.

> "Their condition was halfway between that of free men and that of slaves."[37]
>
> —Classical scholar Arthur Boak on poor tenant farmers who became almost totally dependent on large-estate owners.

When Diocletian took charge of the Empire in the 280s, he was aware of this grim economic reality and earnestly sought to enact reforms. The most famous and widely debated one was the economic

Slaves in ancient Rome receive food for their evening meal. Tenant farmers, or *coloni*, had more rights than slaves but over time they were forced to live under conditions similar to those endured by slaves.

edict he issued in 301, which placed caps on prices and wages. The emperor and his advisors hoped that keeping prices low and stable would make goods and services more affordable to the general population. This grand and well-meaning financial experiment failed, however. The exact reasons remain unclear. But a big one, it seems, is that most Romans resented the government telling them how much they could earn or charge for goods. So they ignored Diocletian's edict or found ways to get around the rules and price caps.

Still another problem that damaged Rome's financial health in the Empire's final two centuries was the fact that its economic system was badly flawed to begin with. Though the realm had long been powerful and well-off, its economic and technological practices could be considered primitive by modern standards. When rotating their crops,

Diocletian Makes His Case

In the preface to his list of fixed prices, issued in 301, Diocletian did his best to make his case to the Roman people why this extreme move—trying to keep prices from going up in order to make goods more affordable and help people avoid falling into debt—was necessary.

> We, who are the protectors of the human race, are agreed, as we view the situation, that decisive legislation is necessary, so that the long-hoped-for solutions which mankind itself could not provide may, by the remedies provided by our foresight, be vouchsafed [granted] for the general betterment of all. We hasten, therefore, to apply the [economic] remedies long demanded by the situation, satisfied that no one can complain that our intervention with [financial] regulations is untimely or unnecessary, trivial or unimportant. . . . For who is so insensitive and so devoid of human feeling that he can be unaware or has not perceived that uncontrolled prices are widespread in the sales taking place in the markets and in the daily life of the cities? Nor is the uncurbed passion for profiteering lessened either by abundant supplies or by fruitful years. It is our pleasure, therefore, that the prices listed in the subjoined [attached] schedule be held in observance in the whole of our Empire. It is our pleasure that anyone who resists the measures of this statute shall be subject to a capital penalty for daring to do so. . . . We therefore exhort [urge] the loyalty of all, so that a regulation instituted for the public good may be observed with willing obedience.

Diocletian, *Edict of Maximum Prices,* in Elsa Graser, ed. and trans., *Corpus Inscriptionum Latinarum,* vol. 3. Philadelphia: American Philological Association, 1940, pp. 801–802.

for example, farmers did not allow enough time for soil nutrients to replenish properly. So soil depletion was a common occurrence. Also, people made cloth on slowly operating looms, spun yarn by hand, and relied too much on the inefficient power of human and animal muscles.

This highly labor-intensive system worked well enough when times were good. But during the immense crises of the fourth and fifth centuries, it came under enormous, unprecedented strain. Rome's methods of agriculture, industrial production, and transport proved inadequate to the Empire's rapidly increasing needs. Eventually, it simply took too many man-hours to produce the amount of food required to feed everyone. As A.H.M. Jones explains, there was not "enough food to rear large families, and many died of malnutrition or of actual starvation."[39]

Barbarians in the Ranks

The largest single share of the unprecedented strain that bore down on the Western Empire in the fourth and fifth centuries consisted of the pressures of invaders along the northern borders. The Romans quite naturally relied on their land army to repel these trespassers. But more and more, Rome's military proved it was not up to the task.

Historians attribute the steep decline of Roman military strength in those two fateful centuries to several causes. They often call one of them the barbarization of the Roman army. This consisted of the admission of increasing numbers of northern European warriors into the army's ranks and the problems that resulted.

The recruitment of non-Romans into the military was not a new phenomenon. It harkened back to the late Republic, although at that time such foreign-born men made up only a very small proportion of the soldiers' ranks. The admission of northern barbarians into the Roman army significantly increased in the late third century, during Diocletian's reign. He recruited several Germanic tribesmen to serve in border areas not far from the lands their tribes then inhabited. The scale of this recruitment was still relatively small, however, and no evidence that it caused any major ill effects has yet been found. As Jones relates, it was only later, when the policy was applied on a much larger scale, that serious troubles arose:

> Such barbarian contingents were harmless and useful, so long as they were sparingly used and went back to their homes beyond the frontier when the campaign was over. The situation entirely changed when Theodosius I, after long and indecisive warfare with the Goths, whom Valens had received into the Empire in 376, gave the entire tribe of Visigoths lands in Greece, allowing

them to remain [permanent residents on Roman lands] under their own king. The Visigoths were ultimately settled in Gaul under the same conditions. And various other barbarian groups that had forced their way into the Empire, such as the Burgundians and the Alans, were given similar terms.[40]

Two different kinds of military barbarization were involved from this period on. One involved the admission of individual barbarian soldiers into Rome's military ranks. In and of itself, evidence suggests, this did not cause a breakdown of discipline, as some scholars used to argue. Most non-Roman recruits learned to follow the rules once they were properly trained. However, it appears that more and more Roman soldiers of this period—including those who were native born—admired the fierce and independent qualities of barbarian fighters. Over time, they came to adopt such qualities, planning to meet ferocity with ferocity on the battlefield. In other words, many native Roman soldiers came to act like barbarian ones.

The other kind of barbarization consisted of Roman leaders enlisting the aid of existing barbarian military units to fight alongside Roman ones against other barbarians. During such campaigns, native Romans further mingled with barbarian warriors, adopting several of their traits in the process. Over time, such trends transformed the Roman army into a less recognizable and reliable fighting force. "Too long and too close association with barbarian warriors, as allies in the Roman army, had ruined the qualities that made Roman armies great," Ferrill contends. As a result, "the Roman army of 440 CE, in the West, had become little more than a barbarian army itself."[41]

> "Barbarian [military] contingents were harmless and useful, so long as they were sparingly used and went back to their homes beyond the frontier when the campaign was over."[40]
>
> —Noted historian A.H.M. Jones.

Other Factors in Military Decline

Another reason the Roman army declined in the Empire's last two centuries was the implementation of a drastic change in overall border

Under Diocletian, every army base in the northern provinces had a strike force of mounted fighters. Soldiers on horseback were tasked with intercepting enemies who had breached border defenses.

strategy. In prior centuries emperors and military generals had opted to make the realm's borders as secure as possible. To that end, they stationed most available soldiers in permanent fortresses on the borders, and intruders seldom broke through these defenses.

Beginning with Diocletian, Constantine, and their immediate successors, however, a new border strategy emerged. Influenced by decades of frequent, random barbarian attacks on the northern borders, it recognized that such assaults were now the rule rather than the exception. Moreover, the new policy conceded that at least some invaders were bound to sometimes penetrate the outer defenses.

So instead of placing most soldiers on the borders, Roman leaders opted for a more in-depth, layered approach. They did keep a few soldiers on the borders. But they also assigned larger numbers of fighters to a few small, fast-moving armies at strategic spots *inside* the northern provinces. These mobile forces, usually having only five hundred to

Entitled to Avoid the Draft

Desperate to recruit Roman citizens into the army, in the 400s the Roman government passed laws that increased conscription across the Empire. There were exemptions, however, and as the late, noted historian Michael Grant pointed out:

> The exempted categories were cripplingly numerous. Hosts of senators, bureaucrats and clergymen were entitled to avoid the draft, and among other groups who escaped [legally] were cooks, bakers and slaves. To draw the rest of the population into the levy, the combing-out process was intensive. Even the men in the emperor's own very extensive estates found themselves called up. Yet other great landlords proved far less cooperative. They were supposed to furnish army recruits in proportion to the size of their lands. But on many occasions they resisted firmly. Moreover, even if they gave way, they exhibited a strong tendency only to send the men they wanted to get rid of. They objected that the levies were a heavy strain on the rural population, which were depleted both in numbers and morale. And indeed there was much truth in this. For, since the inhabitants of the cities were virtually useless as soldiers, that was where the burden fell—on the small farmers and peasants, between the ages of nineteen and thirty-five.

Michael Grant, *The Fall of the Roman Empire.* New York: Macmillan, 1990, pp. 37–38.

one thousand soldiers each, were trained to chase down and intercept any enemy that had recently made it through the border defenses. Diocletian realized that the only way to ensure these mobile fighters were fast enough was to put them on horseback. So he equipped every army base in the northern provinces with a strike force of cavalrymen, or mounted fighters. Once such a unit had done its job, it returned to its base.

Constantine took that concept a step further by keeping some of his mobile forces constantly on the move. They patrolled the northern provinces, going from town to town and region to region. This strategy was designed to make it hard for an invader to know how close such forces were and from where they would counterattack.

What this new strategy did not take into consideration was the enormous size of the barbarian forces that would emerge in the late fourth and fifth centuries. Even when two or more mobile armies joined forces to form a larger unit, it was still too small to overcome a barbarian horde numbering in the tens of thousands. Making matters worse, the increasingly cash-poor Roman government cut back on standard military equipment that had long lent strength to Rome's armies. Body armor was employed less and less, for instance, and in many cases leather caps replaced metal helmets. Military planners also cut back on weapons training.

All of these factors combined to take an awful toll on military efficiency. If the Roman army of Caesar's, Augustus's, or Marcus Aurelius's time had existed in the fifth century, Rome might well have survived. But by the mid-400s, that magnificent military machine had become a mere memory. So the barbarians succeeded and the Western Empire fell.

Which Aspects of Rome Survived to Become Its Legacy?

Focus Questions

1. What were three ways the Romans saw law as a vital foundation of their society, and do these remain a foundation for modern society? Why or why not?
2. How did the Christian church manage to survive Rome's fall, while the imperial government disappeared?
3. How did the Christian church become a combination of guardian and spiritual guide for medieval European civilization in the years following Rome's fall?

In 416 CE poet Rutilius Namatianus, a native of Roman Gaul, published his *Voyage Home to Gaul*. In spite of severe economic problems, the barbarian invasions, and other dire troubles the Empire faced, he did not foresee its collapse. Far from it, his words reveal that he could not conceive of a world that would not be ruled by Rome. That great realm's ongoing reign was "subject to no bounds," he said, "so long as earth shall stand firm and heaven uphold the stars!"[42] It is likely that at that moment in time, the vast majority of Romans, like Namatianus, assumed that Roman civilization as they knew it was fated for immortality. Sooner or later, therefore, the Empire would manage to solve its problems and recover from its recent setbacks.

The Long Perspective of History

Yet a mere six decades later, the Western Roman government, and the Western Empire along with it, ceased to exist. Within a few more generations, moreover—by the mid- to late 500s—Italy's inhabitants no longer thought of themselves as Romans. The roughly thirty thousand residents of the city of Rome itself (who had numbered 1 million or more in Marcus Aurelius's day), still called themselves Romans. But that was only because that city still bore the name Rome. In their view, the venerable ancient race that had erected the Colosseum and other huge, steadily crumbling structures surrounding them was long since gone. Meanwhile, the former Western Roman provinces had become a patchwork quilt of small, culturally backward barbarian kingdoms. For them, too, the once mighty Roman Empire seemed to steadily fade into the past.

What no one could envision at the time was that ancient Rome's western sector was far from dead. Its government, army, provinces, and most other strictly physical aspects had vanished. Yet the *idea* of Rome, with its vibrant undercurrent of Greek culture and thought, remained alive beneath the surface of European culture.

Indeed, the small, scattered kingdoms that now occupied the Western Empire's former lands had absorbed numerous Greco-Roman cultural elements that would profoundly shape their future development. Further, in another comprehensive demonstration of cause and effect, these medieval realms were destined one day to pass on that Greco-Roman legacy to the modern world. Roman civilization "survived the crises" of its decline and fall, the late University of Washington scholar Solomon Katz stated,

> "In the long perspective of history, the survival of Roman civilization, the heritage which generation after generation has accepted, is perhaps more significant than the decline of Rome."[43]
>
> —Former University of Washington scholar Solomon Katz.

and lived on as an integral element of medieval and modern civilization. Rome's triumphs and successes were canceled by her [political and military] failure. But what she accomplished in diverse areas of endeavor was not lost. In the long perspective of history, the survival of Roman civilization, the heritage which generation after generation has accepted, is perhaps more significant than the decline of Rome.[43]

A Guarantee of Freedom

Included in that bountiful heritage are aspects of Roman law, language, and religion. Rome's legal legacy, for example, imparted to later European civilization the fundamental concept that nature possesses certain inherent, unwritten laws. These fair and equitable laws, the Romans held, should apply to people everywhere.

Inspired by the Romans, US founder Thomas Jefferson cited these natural laws in the very first sentence of the Declaration of Independence, which he penned. It was acceptable for the American colonists to become "separate and equal" to Britain, he said, because the "Laws of Nature and of Nature's God entitle them."[44] Roman law also contained the legal concept of trial by jury, which the Greeks had developed to a high level of effectiveness.

Even without Greek legal influences, the Romans had come to see fair, impartial legal concepts and practices as bedrock features of their society. Rome's renowned first-century-BCE senator Marcus Tullius Cicero confirmed that law is "the bond which assures to each of us his honorable life," the "foundation of liberty," and the "fountainhead of

Cicero addresses members of the Roman Senate. Cicero was a strong advocate for a fair, impartial legal system.

justice." Law, Cicero went on, "keeps the heart and mind and initiative and feeling of our nation alive. The state without law would be like a body without [a] brain. It could make no use of its sinews, its blood, or its limbs. The magistrates who administer the law, the judges who act as its spokesmen, [and] all the rest of us who live as its servants, grant it our allegiance as a guarantee of our freedom."[45]

> "The state without law would be like a body without [a] brain."[45]
>
> —First-century-BCE Roman senator Cicero on Roman law.

The Roman Republic in a sense died with Cicero, one of its last great champions. But fortunately for the Roman people, the Empire, which speedily replaced the Republic, inherited its most basic legal concepts. In its five centuries of existence, imperial Rome amassed still more laws, along with lengthy opinions about them by legal experts called jurists. From time to time, these laws and opinions were collected into massive anthologies called legal codes. One was compiled during Diocletian's reign, and in the early fifth century the emperor Theodosius II ordered the creation of another.

After the Western Empire fell, this so-called Theodosian Code did not die with it. Rather, a handful of well-educated individuals in the early medieval European kingdoms kept the code alive, and over time those states used its tenets as models for their own legal systems. In the East at Constantinople, meanwhile, in 528 the emperor Justinian ordered the creation of his own collection of Roman laws. (It incorporated the Theodosian Code.) Called the *Corpus Juris Civilis*, or "Body of Civil Law," it became the basis for eastern Rome's laws until that state fell to the Turks in 1453. Centuries later, the *Corpus*, as it came to be known, was rediscovered in the West.

The manner in which these Roman laws contributed to the development of modern legal systems can be seen in the creation of the United States. The US founders were highly educated men who eagerly absorbed what was then known about Greco-Roman civilization. In particular, they integrated several Roman legal concepts into the framework of their new democracy. This included a major law-making body—the US Senate—based partly on the ancient Roman version.

Latin's Long-Lasting Legacy

Like Rome's legal system, its principal language—Latin—also survived the Empire's fall in the late fifth century. Latin's long-lasting legacy developed in two equally important ways. First, that tongue remained the official language of the Roman Catholic Church, which also survived the fall.

Because Latin continued to be used in the mass and other church ceremonies, over time it underwent little change. Thus, the structure of the Latin used in modern Catholic churches is largely identical to that employed by church officials and other educated Romans in the fourth and fifth centuries. Similarly, this classic form of Latin survived in the early modern scientific classification of animal species. It also continues to be taught in high schools and colleges across the Western world.

The second way that Latin's legacy developed was through its transformation into a series of daughter tongues—the Romance languages. (This version of the word *Romance* came from the Latin phrase *romanice loqui*, meaning "to speak like the Romans.") The development of French is an example of such a transformation. At the time of western Rome's fall, the residents of Gaul spoke an informal version of Latin (as opposed to the formal one used in church). Over the course of several centuries, that Gallic regional variation of Latin gradually changed into French.

Most modern experts agree that about twenty-five separate Romance languages presently exist. In addition to French, they include Italian, Spanish, Portuguese, Romanian, Sicilian, Corsican, Sardinian, Venetian, and Neapolitan. Roughly 800 million people, or around one-eighth of the global population, speak these languages. Another major modern language, English—though technically not a Romance language—features thousands of words that come directly from Latin.

Despite the passage of more than two millennia, therefore, the Romans' native language did not follow them into the void. Instead, the words and phrases they used in both literature and everyday life endure. Moreover, through the Romance languages and English, Latin has embedded itself within the very fabric of the minds, speech, and written materials of more than 1 billion people.

Guardian and Spiritual Guide

The survival of the faith that continues to employ formal Latin in many of its rituals and writings is perhaps the single most striking

Emperor Justinian (pictured in a mosaic dating from around 547) ordered the creation of a collection of laws. These laws, which originated in Constantinople, became the basis for all of the laws of eastern Rome.

aspect of the Roman Empire's legacy to later generations. In retrospect, the long-suffering Christians managed to gain legitimacy and political power in Roman society just in time. Had their belief system not risen to become the realm's leading religion in the fourth and fifth centuries, Rome's traditional pagan faith, with its multiple gods, would likely have remained strongly entrenched. In that case a very different religious scenario might have played out in medieval Europe.

As it happened, however, Christianity spread throughout Roman society and became popular with members of all social classes. That

One of ancient Rome's last noteworthy poets, Rutilius Namatianus, composed the *Voyage Home to Gaul* in 416. His naive assumption that Rome would last forever shows how unthinkable the idea of its fall was only a few years before it actually occurred.

> Listen, O fairest queen of your world, Rome, welcomed amid the starry skies, listen, you mother of men and mother of gods, thanks to your temples we are not far from heaven. [To] you do we chant [the praises of], and shall, while destiny allows, forever chant. None can be safe if forgetful of you. Sooner shall guilty oblivion overwhelm the sun than the honor due to you quit my heart, for your benefits extend as far as the sun's rays, where the circling Ocean-flood bounds the world. For you the very Sun-God who embraces all does revolve. His steeds that rise in your domains he puts in your domains to rest. . . . For nations far apart, you have made a single fatherland. Under your dominion, captivity has meant profit even for those who knew not justice, and by offering to the vanquished a share in your own justice, you have made a city of what was formerly a world. . . . The span [of Rome's reign] which remains [in the future] is subject to no bounds, so long as earth shall stand firm and heaven uphold the stars!

Rutilius Namatianus, *Voyage Home to Gaul,* in *Minor Latin Poets,* vol. 2, trans. J. Wight Duff and Arnold M. Duff. Cambridge, MA: Harvard University Press, 1982, pp. 769, 775.

included the conversion of many of the nobles and other wealthy individuals who had belonged to the imperial court. It was only natural, therefore, that when the imperial government vanished, church leaders, who were also prominent in the court, stepped into the political vacuum that had been created.

This proved to be a wise and crucial move. In the midst of widespread fear, social chaos, and uncertainty caused by western Rome's fall, church leaders furnished some much-needed order. They also encouraged people to have positive feelings about the future. In addition, Rome's fall allowed these leaders, particularly the popes, to assume many of the social and other duties that government officials, especially the emperors, had once performed. As Oxford University scholar Peter Heather puts it:

> The rise of the medieval papacy [the office of the popes] as an overarching authority for the whole of western Christianity is inconceivable without the collapse of the Roman Empire. In the Middle Ages, popes came to play many of the roles within the church that Christian Roman emperors had appropriated to themselves—making laws, calling councils, making or influencing important appointments. Had western emperors of the Roman type still existed, it is inconceivable that popes would have been able to carve out for themselves a position of such independence.[46]

In these ways the church became, in a sense, a combination of guardian and spiritual guide for medieval European civilization. Furthermore, former Roman Christians were not the only people the church aided and watched over. Most of the remaining Roman pagans converted to Christianity within a century or two of the Empire's collapse. In addition, church leaders sent out priests to spread the Christian message to the tribal folk who had overthrown the Western Empire. Soon, almost all of Europe had become Christianized.

"The rise of the medieval papacy as an overarching authority for the whole of western Christianity is inconceivable without the collapse of the Roman Empire."[46]

—Oxford University scholar Peter Heather.

Christianity continued to be successful even after it split into Catholic and Protestant factions in the 1500s. In the three centuries that followed, missionaries from both factions spread across the globe, gathering millions of new converts. Today, upward of thirty-nine thousand separate Christian denominations exist, and Christians number more than 2 billion, making up around a third of the world's total population.

From Firemen to Candy Bars

To these large-scale aspects of Rome's legacy—law, language, and religion—must be added smaller yet still significant ones too numerous

A Roman soldier kneels before the pope. Church leaders provided order and stability during a period of fear, chaos, and uncertainty resulting from western Rome's collapse.

to mention. One of the more widespread and familiar consists of official, professional firefighters. Before Augustus established the Empire, firemen were unpaid slaves owned by rich Roman businessmen. Only when a burning building's owner had agreed to pay the slaves' owner a set fee did those slaves begin fighting the fire. If no deal could be reached, they stood by and watched the structure burn to the ground.

Viewing this arrangement as not only inefficient but also unethical, in 6 CE Augustus set up a professional fire department for the city of Rome. It contained approximately seven thousand firemen called *vigiles*, meaning "watchmen." They were mostly freedmen (former slaves) who received regular salaries, making them paid professionals.

One approach the *vigiles* employed in fighting fires was to form a bucket line, in which water-filled buckets passed from man to man until the last firefighter poured them on the fire. They also tossed

Sources for the Law of Nature

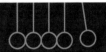

The Romans derived the idea that certain natural laws of equality exist from two sources. One was their own dealings with foreigners, the late, respected scholar R.H. Barrow explains. From these experiences, they "arrived at the notion of an unwritten law of nations." Over time, they equated the law of nations with the law of nature, earlier introduced by the Greeks. Barrow continues:

> Greek philosophy had considered with some care the distinction between what was conventional, arbitrary, fixed by human habits, and crystallized into law, and what was natural, determined by nature according to a large and universal code and smothered by ages of man-made regulations. It was the travels of the Greeks that really started this speculation. For they came across different customs in different lands. Yet they realized that there was some vague and remote resemblance, as though all had come from some common source. This idea of a universal nature was taken up by the [philosophical school of] the Stoics, whose cardinal doctrine was that men should live "according to nature," i.e., according to the [sense of] reason which nature had implanted in man . . . according to the larger reason which animated the world as a whole. Moreover, in late Greek thought there had been doctrines of the unity of mankind, and of the duty of the king to look after and serve the interests of his subjects.

R.H. Barrow, *The Romans.* New York: Penguin, 1982, pp. 211–12.

water-soaked quilts on burning objects. In addition, they had horse-pulled wagons equipped with water reservoirs and portable pumps, the elementary equivalent of today's fire engines. The *vigiles* remained on duty right up to the year 476, when the Roman government ceased to function. Centuries later, some early modern cities began copying Augustus's idea.

Roman names of various kinds also survived Rome's fall and remain in use today. "Abraham Lincoln is a perfect example," University of Louisville historian Robert B. Kebric points out.

> Everyone knows that Abraham is a biblical name, but few would guess that "Lincoln" comes from a corruption of the name of the Roman town of Lindum (*Lin*) Colonia (*Coln*) in Britain. The names of Roman gods [like Jupiter, Saturn, Mars, and Mercury] identify planets, spacecraft, and cars. Our months have Roman names and our calendar is based ultimately on one introduced by Julius Caesar. Saturday was originally Saturn's day. Among our cities there are Romes, Senecas, Ciceros, and Londons, and countless street and business names reflect our Roman heritage. Sports facilities are called "Colosseum" and "Forum," and we buy "Mars" candy bars.[47]

Immortal Rome

Western society inherited many other institutions and services from Rome following its fall. Only a partial list includes postal systems, public hospitals, banking, central heating, daily newspapers, sanitation and sewers, glass windows, apartment buildings, public education, and social welfare benefits. If Rome had survived to the present, these things would still belong to its citizens.

But when the Western Empire fell, they slowly but steadily passed on, at first as ideas, to future generations, including today's. This was how the late, eminent historian of ancient Rome, R.H. Barrow, pictured it. In a sense, he said, "Rome never fell." Rather, it simply "turned into something else." When it ceased to be a political power, it "passed into even greater supremacy as an idea. Rome, with the Latin language, had become immortal."[48]

Introduction: Rome's Fall in the Undergrowth of History

1. Robert Cowley, introduction to *What If: The World's Foremost Military Historians Imagine What Might Have Been*, ed. Robert Cowley. New York: Berkley, 1999, p. xii.
2. Cowley, introduction to Barry S. Strauss, "The Dark Ages Made Lighter," *What If*, p. 72.
3. Strauss, "The Dark Ages Made Lighter," in *What If*, p. 75.
4. Strauss, "The Dark Ages Made Lighter," in *What If*, p. 80.
5. Strauss, "The Dark Ages Made Lighter," in *What If*, pp. 80–81.
6. Cowley, introduction to *What If*, p. xii.

Chapter One: A Brief History of Rome's Rise and Fall

7. Michael Grant, *History of Rome*. New York: Scribner's, 1978, pp. 55–56.
8. Tacitus, *Annals*, published as *Tacitus: The Annals of Imperial Rome*, trans. Michael Grant. New York: Penguin, 1989, p. 32.
9. Edward Gibbon, *The Decline and Fall of the Roman Empire*, ed. David Womersley, vol. 1. New York: Penguin, 1994, pp. 101, 103.
10. Michael Grant, *The Fall of the Roman Empire*. New York: Macmillan, 1990, p. 3.
11. Gibbon, *The Decline and Fall of the Roman Empire*, vol. 1, p. 482.

Chapter Two: Did the Barbarian Invasions Cause Rome's Fall?

12. Adrian Goldsworthy, *How Rome Fell: Death of a Superpower*. New Haven, CT: Yale University Press, 2010, p. 1.
13. Goldsworthy, *How Rome Fell*, p. 1.
14. Goldsworthy, *How Rome Fell*, p. 1.
15. Grant, *The Fall of the Roman Empire*, p. xi.
16. Barry Cunliffe, *Rome and the Barbarians*. New York: Walck, 1975, p. 124.
17. Gibbon, *The Decline and Fall of the Roman Empire*, vol. 2, p. 512.

18. Suetonius, *Lives of the Twelve Caesars*, published as *The Twelve Caesars*, trans. Robert Graves, rev. Michael Grant. New York: Penguin, 1979, p. 65.
19. Appian, *Roman History*, trans. Horace White. Cambridge, MA: Harvard University Press, 1972, p. 11.
20. Ammianus Marcellinus, *History*, published as *The Later Roman Empire, A.D. 354–378*, trans. and ed. Walter Hamilton. New York: Penguin, 1986, p. 435.
21. Cunliffe, *Rome and the Barbarians*, p. 124.
22. Cunliffe, *Rome and the Barbarians*, p. 124.

Chapter Three: Did Internal Disunities Fatally Weaken Rome?

23. Grant, *The Fall of the Roman Empire*, p. 23.
24. Gibbon, *The Decline and Fall of the Roman Empire*, vol. 1, p. 595.
25. A.H.M. Jones, *The Decline of the Ancient World*. London: Routledge, 2014, pp. 262–63.
26. Quoted in J.F. O'Sullivan, trans., *The Writing of Salvian the Presbyter*. Washington, DC: Catholic University of America Press, 1977, pp. 140–41.
27. Grant, *The Fall of the Roman Empire*, p. 60.
28. Ammianus, *The Later Roman Empire*, p. 48.
29. Harold Mattingly, *The Man on the Roman Street*. New York: Norton, 1976, p. 147.
30. Grant, *The Fall of the Roman Empire*, pp. 72–73.
31. Jones, *The Decline of the Ancient World*, p. 25.
32. Gibbon, *The Decline and Fall of the Roman Empire*, vol. 1, p. 481.

Chapter Four: Did Economic and Military Factors Destroy Rome?

33. Arther Ferrill, *The Fall of the Roman Empire: The Military Explanation*. New York: Thames and Hudson, 1995, p. 22.
34. Ferrill, *The Fall of the Roman Empire*, p. 12.
35. Ferrill, *The Fall of the Roman Empire*, p. 12.
36. Anonymous oration from the fourth century, in *Roman Civilization: Selected Readings*, ed. Naphtali Lewis and Meyer Reinhold, vol. 2. New York: Columbia University Press, 1990, p. 432.

37. Arthur Boak and William G. Sinnegin, *A History of Rome to 565 A.D.* New York: Macmillan, 1965, pp. 455–56.

38. Quoted in Lewis and Reinhold, *Roman Civilization: Selected Readings*, vol. 2, p. 437.

39. Jones, *The Decline of the Ancient World*, p. 366.

40. Jones, *The Decline of the Ancient World*, p. 215.

41. Ferrill, *The Fall of the Roman Empire*, pp. 84–85, 140.

Chapter Five: Which Aspects of Rome Survived to Become Its Legacy?

42. Rutilius Namatianus, *Voyage Home to Gaul*, in *Minor Latin Poets*, trans. J. Wight Duff and Arnold M. Duff, vol. 2. Cambridge, MA: Harvard University Press, 1982, p. 775.

43. Solomon Katz, *The Decline of Rome and the Rise of Medieval Europe.* Ithaca, NY: Cornell University Press, 1966, p. 139.

44. National Archives, "The Declaration of Independence." www.archives.gov.

45. Cicero, *Pro Cluentio*, in *Cicero: Murder Trials*, trans. Michael Grant. New York: Penguin, 1990, pp. 216–17.

46. Peter Heather, *The Fall of the Roman Empire: A New History of Rome and the Barbarians.* New York: Oxford University Press, 2006, p. 442.

47. Robert B. Kebric, *Roman People.* New York: McGraw-Hill, 2005, pp. E-3–E-4.

48. R.H. Barrow, *The Romans.* New York: Penguin, 1982, p. 204.

Books

Peter Brown, *Through the Eye of a Needle: Wealth, the Fall of Rome, and the Making of Christianity in the West, 350–550 AD.* Princeton, NJ: Princeton University Press, 2014.

Averil Cameron, *The Later Roman Empire: A.D. 284–430.* Cambridge, MA: Harvard University Press, 1993.

Neil Christie, *The Fall of the Western Empire: Archaeology, History, and the Decline of Rome.* New York: Bloomsbury Academic, 2011.

Arther Ferrill, *The Fall of the Roman Empire: The Military Explanation.* New York: Thames and Hudson, 1995.

Charles Freeman, *Egypt, Greece, and Rome: Civilizations of the Ancient Mediterranean.* Oxford: Oxford University Press, 2014.

Edward Gibbon, *The Decline and Fall of the Roman Empire.* Edited by David Womersley. 3 vols. New York: Penguin, 2001.

Adrian Goldsworthy, *How Rome Fell: Death of a Superpower.* New Haven, CT: Yale University Press, 2010.

Michael Grant, *Constantine the Great: The Man and His Times.* New York: Barnes and Noble, 2009.

Peter Heather, *Empires and Barbarians: The Fall of Rome and the Birth of Europe.* New York: Oxford University Press, 2012.

Peter Heather, *The Fall of the Roman Empire: A New History of Rome and the Barbarians.* New York: Oxford University Press, 2006.

A.H.M. Jones, *The Later Roman Empire, 284–602.* 3 vols. Baltimore, MD: Johns Hopkins University Press, 1986.

Tracey Turner, *Hard Nuts to Crack: Ancient Rome.* London: A and C Black, 2014.

Websites

And Now for the News, *Atlantic* (www.theatlantic.com/magazine /archive/1997/03/and-now-for-the-news/376802). Robert D. Kaplan, a widely respected correspondent for the *Atlantic*, explains why, after the passage of two centuries, Gibbon's masterwork remains relevant and crucial to modern studies of Rome and its fall.

The Fall of Rome, BBC (www.bbc.co.uk/history/ancient/romans /fallofrome_article_01.shtml). Historian Peter Heather, one of the world's leading authorities on Rome's fall, discusses some of the major causes of that seminal event.

The Fall of Rome, EyeWitness to History (www.eyewitnessto history.com/fallofrome.htm). Provides an English translation of Saint Jerome's famous remarks after learning of large-scale barbarian intrusions in the early 400s.

Reasons for the Fall of Rome, About Education (http://ancient history.about.com/od/fallofrome/tp/022509FallofRomeReasons. htm). Researcher in classical history N.S. Gill presents eight of the often-cited reasons for the fall of western Rome and provides some solid suggestions for further reading.

Why Empires Fall: From Ancient Rome to Putin's Russia, *New Statesman* (www.newstatesman.com/politics/2014/05/why-empires -fall-ancient-rome-putins-russia). British historian Tom Holland penned this thoughtful May 2014 article that explores how Rome's fall was part of a larger historical trend.

Historian and award-winning author Don Nardo has written numerous books about the ancient world, its peoples, and their cultures, including volumes on the Babylonians, Assyrians, Persians, Minoans, Greeks, Etruscans, Romans, Carthaginians, and others. In addition, he is the author of single-volume encyclopedias on ancient Mesopotamia, ancient Greece, ancient Rome, and Greek and Roman mythology. Nardo, who also composes and arranges orchestral music, lives with his wife, Christine, in Massachusetts.